THE CLIMATE CRISIS IN THE UPPER MIDWEST

by Julie Kentner

FOCUS READERS®
NAVIGATOR

WWW.FOCUSREADERS.COM

Copyright © 2024 by Focus Readers®, Lake Elmo, MN 55042. All rights reserved. No part of this book may be reproduced or utilized in any form or by any means without written permission from the publisher.

Focus Readers is distributed by North Star Editions:
sales@northstareditions.com | 888-417-0195

Produced for Focus Readers by Red Line Editorial.

Content Consultant: Michael Notaro, PhD, Director of the Nelson Institute Center for Climatic Research, University of Wisconsin–Madison

Photographs ©: Shutterstock Images, cover, 1, 8–9, 14–15, 21; Nati Harnik/AP Images, 4–5; Chris Machian/Omaha World-Herald/AP Images, 7; Red Line Editorial, 11; NOAA/Suomi NPP/NOAA's Environmental Visualization Laboratory/NASA, 13; Dr. L. Scott Mills/North Carolina State University/USGS, 17; Carlyn Iverson/Science Source, 19; Jim West/Science Source, 22–23; iStockphoto, 25; Jessie Wardarski/AP Images, 27; Katie Flenker/Alamy, 29

Library of Congress Cataloging-in-Publication Data
Library of Congress Cataloging-in-Publication Data is available on the Library of Congress website.

ISBN
978-1-63739-637-7 (hardcover)
978-1-63739-694-0 (paperback)
978-1-63739-802-9 (ebook pdf)
978-1-63739-751-0 (hosted ebook)

Printed in the United States of America
Mankato, MN
082023

ABOUT THE AUTHOR
Julie Kentner is a writer who loves history, geography, archaeology, travel, and research. She lives with her husband and their cats.

TABLE OF CONTENTS

CHAPTER 1
Iowa Floods 5

CHAPTER 2
Upper Midwest Climate 9

CHAPTER 3
Crisis on the Lakes and Plains 15

THAT'S AMAZING!
Stephanie Salgado 20

CHAPTER 4
Fighting the Crisis 23

Focus on the Upper Midwest • 30
Glossary • 31
To Learn More • 32
Index • 32

CHAPTER 1

IOWA FLOODS

The upper Midwest received lots of snow during the winter of 2018–19. In March 2019, Iowa warmed up quickly. Then it started to rain. The rain melted the snow. However, the ground was still frozen. As a result, the rainwater and melted snow could not soak into the ground.

Floods in March 2019 made some roads in Iowa unusable.

Instead, water flowed over the ground into creeks and rivers. Those bodies of water flooded. The water tore apart many **levees** across Iowa. The flooding was especially bad along the Missouri River. People in several towns had to leave their homes. The costs of the damage topped

FLOOD DAMAGE

Floods can cause a variety of problems. They can damage a community's infrastructure. Infrastructure includes buildings, bridges, and roads. It also includes power lines, pipes, and wells. Sometimes, floodwater seeps into wells. If that happens, drinking water can become unsafe. That's because floodwater often contains poisonous substances. They can make people sick.

Many rural areas in Iowa were hit extremely hard by the 2019 floods.

$1.6 billion. Three years later, some communities were still replacing levees.

Research links these types of events to **climate change**. Scientists expect flooding to continue to increase across the region.

CHAPTER 2

UPPER MIDWEST CLIMATE

Weather involves what happens from day to day. It includes temperature, **precipitation**, and many other conditions. Climate measures these things, too. But climate tracks weather patterns over many years.

The upper Midwest is in the middle of North America. It includes Minnesota,

Flat landscapes and frequent precipitation make much of the upper Midwest good for farming.

Wisconsin, Iowa, and Michigan. It is known for its flat land and rolling hills.

No mountain ranges lie to the region's north or south. For this reason, the upper Midwest receives cold gusts from the Arctic. The Arctic is a very cold region near the North Pole. The upper Midwest also gets warm, humid air from the Gulf of Mexico. This air often leads to heavy rains and flooding. Getting air from both the Arctic and Gulf also means the region has a wide range of temperatures. Summers are often hot. Winters can be very cold.

However, the upper Midwest is also home to several Great Lakes. The Great

Lakes are the largest freshwater system in the world. Water warms up and cools down more slowly than land. As a result, areas along the Great Lakes have milder seasons.

THE UPPER MIDWEST

The Great Lakes affect precipitation as well. In late fall and winter, cold air passes over the lakes from the north. The air is colder and drier than the water. This temperature and moisture difference

THE MENOMINEE NATION

The **Indigenous** Menominee (Muh-*nahm*-uh-nee) people have lived in the upper Midwest for thousands of years. Wisconsin became a US state in 1848. Six years later, the Menominee signed an agreement with the United States. They kept some land in Wisconsin. A forest covered most of it. To this day, the Menominee produce lumber **sustainably**. They use only old and sick trees. This practice allows the young trees to grow. It keeps the forest healthy for future generations.

A satellite image shows lake-effect snow across the Great Lakes.

helps produce tons of snow. This is known as the lake effect. In the upper Midwest, parts of Michigan and Wisconsin receive the most lake-effect snow. Minnesota also receives plenty of winter snow. However, much of the region's precipitation falls in summer. Summer storms are common in the upper Midwest.

CHAPTER 3

CRISIS ON THE LAKES AND PLAINS

Human activity is the main cause of the climate crisis. People burn huge amounts of **fossil fuels**. They use fossil fuels for many reasons. Power plants burn them to produce electricity and heat homes. People also use fossil fuels to drive cars and trucks. These activities release additional **greenhouse gases**

Rising temperatures from climate change tend to more greatly affect cities.

15

into the atmosphere. These gases are warming up the planet. They are causing climate change.

    This crisis is affecting the upper Midwest. Average temperatures are rising. In general, the region's winters have warmed more than its summers.

    Higher temperatures are leading to other changes. For example, snow protects the roots of trees during the winter. But warmer winters mean there is less snow on the ground. Thin, shallow tree roots might freeze. This can slow tree growth. Warmer temperatures also mean some insects can survive over the winter. New types may move into the region.

Snowshoe hares' white fur blends in with snow. Less snow makes it easier for predators to find them.

These pests can harm trees. So, they are known as invasive species.

The region's precipitation is changing, too. The snow season is getting shorter. Winters are likely to have more rain and less snow. Springs are likely to have more rain. This change could lead to more flooding.

Flooding has a variety of impacts. For instance, farming is important throughout the upper Midwest. But floods may force farmers to plant their crops later in the spring. That can lead to a shorter growing season and fewer crops produced. These changes can harm food supplies and local economies.

Climate change is also impacting the Great Lakes. The lakes are becoming warmer. The warmer lake temperatures are leading to many changes. Certain fish can now survive farther north. They move to areas where cold-water fish are. Then cold-water fish have to compete with the other fish for food.

The lake whitefish is one fish threatened by loss of ice cover on the Great Lakes.

Parts of the Great Lakes also freeze over during the winter. This is called ice cover. The ice protects the eggs of some fish. But warmer temperatures have greatly lowered ice cover. As a result, the eggs have less protection. Scientists expect those fish numbers to drop as a result.

THAT'S AMAZING!

STEPHANIE SALGADO

Stephanie Salgado was born and raised in Honduras. Her family moved to Wisconsin in 2015. When she was in high school, she helped write a book. It featured stories of **immigration** to Wisconsin.

Salgado soon connected these experiences to climate change. She found that the crisis affects communities of color differently. These communities often have fewer resources than white communities. This makes it harder to prepare for the effects of climate change.

In response, Salgado began working for climate justice. She helped lead several groups at the University of Wisconsin–Madison. She helped organize a youth march to raise awareness about

Stephanie Salgado worked to get the University of Wisconsin to stop putting money toward fossil fuels.

the crisis. In 2019, she also joined the Wisconsin Governor's Task Force on Climate Change. She was the youngest member of the team.

CHAPTER 4

FIGHTING THE CRISIS

Switching to renewable energy sources can slow climate change. Renewable energy sources do not run out. They also produce far less greenhouse gases than burning fossil fuels. One example of renewable energy is solar power. It uses energy from the sun. Sunlight shines on

A solar farm produces electricity in Detroit, Michigan.

23

solar panels. The panels turn the light's energy into electricity.

Groups large and small are building more solar panels. In 2021, workers completed a field of solar panels in Fitchburg, Wisconsin. The city, the state, a university, and several companies all worked together. The groups that helped all received solar power.

Wind is another source of renewable energy. Wind turbines are machines that make electricity when they rotate. A large group of wind turbines is called a wind farm.

In Iowa, companies work with landowners to build wind farms.

Iowa is home to thousands of wind turbines.

Wind generated 58 percent of Iowa's electricity in 2021. That was the highest use of wind power for any state.

However, climate change is already here. For this reason, people must also adapt. Adaptation means making changes to deal with a new situation. Climate adaptation means making changes that reduce the harms of the climate crisis.

25

Many groups are working on adaptation. One example is the Great Lakes Climate Adaptation Network (GLCAN). This group is studying the

ANISHINAABE PEOPLES

Climate change is impacting Anishinaabe (Ah-nish-ih-*nah*-bay) peoples. These Indigenous nations live across Michigan, Wisconsin, and Minnesota. One impact is on *manoomin*, or wild rice. Many Anishinaabe people depend on this food. *Manoomin* grows in shallow water. But it can die if water levels are too high or too low. Floods and invasive species are also threats. Many tribes are adapting. Some are planting different trees in wetlands. The trees could help prevent flooding and protect *manoomin*.

Anishinaabe members of the Leech Lake Band of Ojibwe harvest *manoomin* on Leech Lake in Minnesota.

climate crisis in the Great Lakes area. GLCAN looked at the climate science. Then it studied specific cities in the region. It examined the climate risks each city faced. Using this information, GLCAN wrote reports. Leaders of those cities could use those reports. They could better plan for the future.

27

Flooding is a common threat in the upper Midwest. Areas are taking many steps to adapt. In Detroit, Michigan, workers are building large tanks under streets. These tanks collect water from storms. Then the tanks release the water slowly into the sewer system. This helps reduce flooding in the city.

Rural areas also face extreme floods. In Iowa, people are restoring native wetlands. They are digging ponds near farms. Ponds and wetlands can hold extra water from storms.

Young people can help. They can become citizen scientists. Citizen scientists are regular people who help

Nearly 95 percent of Iowa's native wetlands were drained after settlers took the land from Indigenous peoples.

scientists do research. They gather data where they live. The data can help people understand local climate impacts.

Students can talk to teachers and other students. They can ask their schools to be more climate-friendly. Young people can also write to and call local leaders. They can explain why climate action matters.

FOCUS ON
THE UPPER MIDWEST

Write your answers on a separate piece of paper.

1. Write a paragraph describing the main ideas of Chapter 4.

2. How could you help your area adapt to climate change?

3. What is the term for the way the Great Lakes produce more precipitation?

> **A.** lake effect
> **B.** invasive species
> **C.** native wetlands

4. How do wetlands help prevent flooding?

> **A.** People can hide in wetlands during storms.
> **B.** Wetlands help reduce strong storms.
> **C.** Wetlands can store large amounts of water.

Answer key on page 32.

GLOSSARY

climate change
A human-caused global crisis involving long-term changes in Earth's temperature and weather patterns.

fossil fuels
Energy sources that come from the remains of plants and animals that died long ago.

greenhouse gases
Gases that trap heat in Earth's atmosphere, causing climate change.

immigration
The process of moving to a new country to live permanently.

Indigenous
Native to a region, or belonging to ancestors who lived in a region before colonists arrived.

levees
Walls built from earthen materials to stop floodwaters.

precipitation
Water that falls from clouds to the ground. It can be in the form of rain, hail, sleet, or snow.

sustainably
Done in a way that does not harm or use up a resource.

TO LEARN MORE

BOOKS

Cooke, Joanna. *Using Wind Turbines to Fight Climate Change*. Lake Elmo, MN: Focus Readers, 2023.

Harman, Alice. *Climate Change and How We'll Fix It*. New York: Union Square Kids, 2021.

Vernon, Jane. *Minnesota*. Minneapolis: Abdo Publishing, 2023.

NOTE TO EDUCATORS

Visit **www.focusreaders.com** to find lesson plans, activities, links, and other resources related to this title.

INDEX

Anishinaabe peoples, 26

Detroit, Michigan, 11, 28

Fitchburg, Wisconsin, 24
flooding, 6–7, 10, 17–18, 26, 28

Great Lakes, 10–12, 18–19, 27

Great Lakes Climate Adaptation Network (GLCAN), 26–27

ice cover, 19
invasive species, 17, 26
Iowa, 5–6, 10–11, 24–25, 28

lake-effect snow, 12–13

Menominee people, 12
Michigan, 10–11, 13, 26, 28
Minnesota, 9, 11, 13, 26
Missouri River, 6, 11

Salgado, Stephanie, 20–21
solar power, 23–24

wind power, 24–25
Wisconsin, 10–13, 20–21, 24, 26

Answer Key: 1. Answers will vary; 2. Answers will vary; 3. A; 4. C